Girl Like Me

Girl Like Me

"Walking with a Father who loves with an unfathomable love and pursues us even to the darkest pits, rescuing us from ourselves."

MARCIA A. YETMAN

Girl Like Me

Copyright © 2021 Marcia A. Yetman

All rights reserved. No part of this publication may be reproduced, distributed, or transmitted in any form or by any means, without prior written permission.

Published by Equip Press, Colorado Springs, CO

Scripture quotations marked (NIV) are taken from the Holy Bible, New International Version. Copyright © 1973, 1978, 1984, 2011 by Biblica, Inc.® Used by permission. All rights reserved worldwide.

Scripture quotations marked (NRSV) are taken from the New Revised Standard Version Bible, copyright © 1989 the Division of Christian Education of the National Council of the Churches of Christ in the United States of America. Used by permission. All rights reserved.

First Edition: 2021
Girl Like Me / Marcia A. Yetman
Paperback ISBN: 978-1-951304-72-0
eBook ISBN: 978-1-951304-73-7

Contents

Introduction   7

1. Hopeless and Helpless   9

2. A Defining Moment   17

3. The Road Ahead   25

4. Putting the Pieces Back Together   41

5. Lessons from My Father   45

6. A Work in Progress   53

   Special Dedication   59

Introduction

Like many others, I have come to understand that life consists of a series of well-designed battles. Our success partly depends on how well we fight. It is also just as important not to lose sight of the lessons learned from those battles we may have lost.

I dedicate this work to the heroes of this life who have risen from the ashes of what we call failure and have remained standing. This is for the countless sisters, girls, mothers, wives, and friends who have contemplated making or have made life-altering decisions from a place of fear, anger, abandonment, rejection, or hopelessness. For that young man, husband, son, and father who watched helplessly as someone else made a decision that bore a hole in your heart. Maybe today, you are living with regrets—you may feel emotionally crippled. Your heart has become cold, and sometimes it feels almost lifeless. I understand that place.

Why the title *Girl Like Me*? This phrase was dropped into my spirit years ago while having a conversation with my Father. I heard this in the depths of my soul— "There are many **girls like you** who need to know how to rise from a fall and live again." I didn't know what to do with it. I wrote down the words *Girl Like Me.* Over the years, I would see those words in my mind's eye and ponder them in my heart. So here we are today. This is for all the "girls like me" and others walking through the recovery and restoration process.

Join me as I journey through one of my deep, dark seasons. Words captured in a little black and white notebook were left untouched for twenty years as I chronicled my deepest thoughts, fears, and emotions to a Father who loves with an unfathomable love and pursues us even to the darkest pits. During my journey, one of my college girlfriends asked me (almost in awe), "How do you do this?" I said one word—*Jesus*. There is light after the darkness…with Jesus.

Looking Back Twenty Years

For many of us, 2020 was a year of reflection. Throughout most of my life, I have journaled frequently—documenting some of the most challenging periods of my life. One morning, I randomly picked up a black and white notebook that I had written in for many months in the year 2000. Now twenty years later, I started to gloss over what I had walked through during that season of my life. I felt some very raw emotions as I started to read. I had never shared this with anyone up to that point. I heard a still small voice saying, "It's time…." Time to let others know there is a loving Father who never abandons you—even at your most vulnerable. He wants us to be bare, naked, and unashamed before Him. He desires "truth in the inward parts."

In 2000, I had become pregnant as an unwed mother, the second time around—*in church*. This time around, I didn't want to—I couldn't do this again! There was no place on my vision board for this slice of reality. I was supposedly a smart, educated, saved young woman. How could I have embarrassed my Father like this?? How could I have done this—again? Shame, fear, and hopelessness weighed me down. I wouldn't carry this child—I couldn't carry this child! Here's my journey….

1

Hopeless and Helpless

FEBRUARY 18, 2000

This was the moment I confirmed that I was pregnant. After the doctor shared the results with me, she asked what my plans were. I couldn't verbally respond. I had never felt so hopeless and helpless—I just burst into tears. I don't remember the details of the conversation, but I remember a seed was planted in me that day. I had options!! Before this day, I had never, ever entertained the idea of abortion once. I plunged into a dark place mentally and emotionally. In the depth of despair, however, part of me refused to die. That part of me that knew that MY Heavenly Father loved me and would listen. So I began to write:

"Questions in Darkness"

> *Who said there's light at the end of the tunnel?*
> *Whoever found a pot of gold at the end of the rainbow?*
> *Who said there's always a calm after the storm?*
> *Is it true that if I make my bed in hell—Lord, you are there?*

Where is the peace that they say is in the valley?
What does it mean when it says "in your weakness, His strength is made perfect"?
How is it that I can't understand that "all things work together for good…"?
This is a very dark moment in my soul.
I was wondering— "Can You hold me now?"

LESSONS LEARNED:

There are so many things about life that we may never fully understand. Our limitations sometimes do not make us good candidates to fully grasp life's mysteries. A few years ago, in my conversation with God, I found myself in a place where I was very critical of someone. The Lord lovingly reminded me that I do not know enough to make a judgment call on that person's life or choices. This brings me to an experience I had maybe a year before I found myself pregnant and unwed.

I was home one afternoon when a 'sister' called and asked if she could come over. When she walked into my apartment, I could see she was not in a good place. She proceeded to tell me that she needed to share something that had been weighing heavy on her. She continued to explain that the Lord told her to come and talk to me. I said okay—I'm good at listening. She went on to tearfully share her story, one that was very painful for her to share. When she was in her early twenties, she had gotten pregnant twice and had ended the pregnancies twice. She was a young professional at that time, and single motherhood didn't fit into her or her family's vision for her life. She did not want to marry these men. She thought that was the best decision at the time. Now she was older, a successful professional, and had never gotten married or had children. The regret was greatly consuming her; it was too painful to bear alone.

Now she had a relationship with the Lord, and it seemed as if He wanted to bring healing to her past. Sometimes, for wounds to heal, they need to be exposed and the false bandage we cover them with must be ripped off. We cover our wounds with things, people, accolades, and trophies—anything we can achieve or accomplish to numb or suppress the memories of those not-so-great choices in our past.

I listened and prayed with her. I knew God wanted her to be free to embrace His forgiveness and to move on. I felt that was accomplished that day—she appeared lighter, as if a boulder had rolled off her back. Funny, when she left, I was a bit puzzled. I remember asking the Lord in passing why He chose me. Why did you send her to me? Did she really hear from You? I didn't see the connection or why I was a good fit. I had never considered abortion or had any experience with it. I shrugged it off as one of those things I don't understand. The Lord didn't answer me.

Now here I was a year or so later, standing at this crossroad. That day certainly came back to me, and it all made sense then. The Lord HAD sent her to me that day—He knew I would one day contemplate ending a pregnancy. My limited mind had no idea, so I questioned why God would send her to me. He reminded me that some regrets are overwhelmingly painful. I have learned that God does nothing without a purpose. We will not always understand the ways of the Lord—things don't always make sense. It's a good practice to trust God with the question marks and not be quick to make judgment calls. We don't know enough.

> *"...Oh, how great are God's... wisdom and knowledge! How impossible it is for us to understand his decisions and his ways! For who can know the Lord's thoughts? Who knows enough to give him advice?"*
> **(Rom. 11: 33-34 NLT)**

FEBRUARY 29, 2000

Aloneness—real or imagined- is a real place. This is especially true when you struggle with life-altering decisions. I found that, for me, it was also a choice. I chose not to let others in. The truth is—I didn't want their voices in my head. Looking back—I knew what God wanted. Sometimes the conflict in decision-making arises because we want to do what we want to do.

"Alone"

> *Why is it that I always feel so alone at these critical points in my life?*
> *These decisions, moves, choices that I am literally forced to make on my own get overwhelming at times.*
> *Why do I get so lonely at these times?*
> *No one to help make these decisions—no second opinion.*
> *Just a feeling that I must do what I must.*
> *I get so tired in my mind at these times—my body feels worn.*
> *At times I want to walk away...run away...to a place where I*

need not think, act, or be.
A place of total oblivion to the world around –
Where I neither act nor react to situations around me.
Now I want to walk away from everything...leave it all behind...escape
To a place where this aloneness can soothe and calm the storm in my soul.

LESSONS LEARNED:

Being alone sometimes is a part of the refining process. God may well separate us from those voices that would normally be loud in our heads. It is in aloneness at times that we are silent long enough to hear what God is saying. We learn to separate God's ways from our own preconceived notions, from the dictates of culture and even religion. We get to hear what God's directives are for our personal situation. I have learned that the Lord does not lead by the truths of psychology or man's philosophy. It is true that the foolishness of God is wiser than man (**1 Cor. 1:25**). In the silence of our aloneness, God brings to light His truth. Sometimes His truths don't make sense to the natural man, but we never go wrong when we obey them.

MARCH 1, 2000

I remember sitting by the beach one day—my soul in turmoil. The sky was blue, the beach was half-empty, the water was calm and soothing. As I looked at the beautiful ocean meeting the blue skies way off in the distance, I heard a quiet voice encouraging me to walk into the water. To walk until I reached the end—wherever that was. Death can sometimes feel like a welcoming place of escape when we find it difficult to cope. That was how I felt this day. The truth is—it is never the answer. That desire does not come from God.

"Death"

> *Sometimes death feels like a safe haven.*
> *Sometimes I feel led to walk into it, but who knows where it will end.*
> *I feel a tug in my heart…*
> *A longing for something else.*
> *A strong desire for solitude…to be left alone*
> *To be drawn into a quietness where I hear no voices –*
> *No questions, no conflicts—no fear.*
> *Sometimes death feels like the comfort I need.*
> *I want to be left alone—not seen by anyone*
> *No expectations of me—no requirements*
> *Just let me be—until I find myself.*
> *Sometimes death seems so warm and inviting*
> *But will it bring me life?*

LESSONS LEARNED:

We are very complex beings with powerful emotions and desires. If those emotions are not submitted to God, they can take us out in a minute. How many lives have been destroyed by misled passion? Not everything that feels or looks good is God. God does use our emotions

—there is no argument about that. However, time has taught me that I must weigh what I feel against God's truth.

I'd never had a battle with suicidal thoughts, but I know they are real. At that moment, I felt a need to just fly away, to just escape. That seemed to be the best way out. I don't understand everything about the struggle with suicidal ideation, but I do understand how one can get there. There are many ways to deal with this enemy of life. Whatever you are led to do, always remember the truth of God overrides the enemy's lies every time.

God will never go against His own Word. Remember, the enemy is very deceptive. He can influence us with a false sense of peace about something totally against God's will. We have heard the song "How Can Something So Wrong Feel So Right?" The true test can never be what we feel. It must be what God says.

REFLECTIONS

2

A Defining Moment

MARCH 16, 2000

This was the moment I decided I would end this pregnancy. I knew my Father wouldn't approve of it, but I didn't have the strength to do the right thing. Troubled and weak …Have you ever found yourself here at this place? Knowing what is right but not having the strength to do it.

"Troubled"

> *Have you ever had your life thrown into total chaos?*
> *Not knowing if you are coming or going?*
> *Have you ever had all your dreams dashed and the pieces scattered?*
> *Have you ever felt like you just can't come through?*
> *Like you've made such a mess this time, you can't recover?*
> *Have you ever sunk so low that you wonder what can pick you up?*
> *Did anyone ever do it this bad?*
> *Have you ever wondered what God thinks about you?*
> *Have you ever thought that He gave up on you?*

That He turned His back said, "You made your bed, now lie in it"?
Have you ever felt His silence? Isn't that a frightening feeling?
He says nothing and you wonder...
Have you ever made up your mind to do something you know was a gross sin because you thought it was the only way out?
Have you ever had your heart gripped by fear and hopelessness?
That the faith you need refuses to rise up in you?
Have you ever felt you are on a road—a destructive path?
You don't want to be there but –
Somehow you don't have what it takes to turn around?
Have you ever wondered if you'll make it when all is said and done?
Have you ever wondered about the depth of God's love and forgiveness?
Can it reach down and pick you up no matter the depth of iniquity and darkness that engulfs you?
Have you ever had these thoughts?
Well—I have...
Troubled One

LESSONS LEARNED:

Only when I read this could I take myself back to that place of utter conflict and turmoil. I felt storm-battered and completely conflicted. This is a place I don't ever want to visit again. The most frightening thing for me was my Father's apparent silence—NOTHING. I never felt so abandoned. Nevertheless, I kept talking. He was my only solace—I knew He was listening. I kept pouring out my soul.

I have since learned that when He appears to be silent, that's when an amazing work is being done in those deep places. There was a battle raging for my soul, and He never stopped fighting for me. I don't have to feel it or sense His presence—I just need to know and believe that He never abandons a child who cries out to Him. He is the perfect Father. It is true that 'in my weakness, His strength is made perfect.'

The more I get to know the God I serve, the more I realize that my efforts to make me 'good' almost always end in frustration. My part in the process is to agree that I am flawed and imperfect—in need of redemption and restoration. I have also found that even when I don't want to change, when I like my mess, my Father is simply waiting for me to speak truth. Numerous times I have found myself in a place where I don't want what God wants. This usually results in what we call a struggle. This is where I tell God exactly that—I don't want to, or I don't want that.

I don't know how to change my desires, so I ask Him to do what I can't do for myself. This keeps me in a place of continued dependence on Him. I want to want what He wants for me, but I don't know how to get 'me' to that place. He has never failed to do that work in my inner man. It remains a mystery to me today. How does He do that? Give Him the broken, flawed, messed-up 'you' and watch the mind-boggling transformation that He does through the power of His Holy Spirit!

If I have anything worth sharing, this is it! Change begins when I come before my Father in truth and from a place void of pretense and hypocrisy. I don't have to always say what I think He wants to hear—He already knows my heart. God responds to us not necessarily based on what we say but what's in our hearts. That part of us that only He knows. That is why He is the just Judge—His way is perfect.

In a matter of 24 hours, I watched my Father change my desire to end the life of an unborn child to one of 'wanting what God wants.'

He does hear you; He does see your heart! He wants to give you beauty for ashes.

> *"For the mountains shall depart and the hills be removed, but My kindness shall not depart from you, nor shall My covenant of peace be removed," Says the LORD, who has mercy on you. "O you afflicted one, tossed with tempest, and not comforted, behold, I will lay your stones with colorful gems, and lay your foundations with sapphires."*
> **(Isaiah 54:10-11NKJV)**

MARCH 17, 2000

I'll never forget this day. It was St. Patrick's Day—a dark, gloomy day in NYC, both literally and figuratively. This was the day I planned to go back to the doctor to end this pregnancy. Funny, I took a bus—alone. As I sat about two or three seats behind the driver, I started to talk to the only One I knew who would 'get me' right now—my Father. With brokenness and weariness in my soul, I said, 'Father, I am about to do something that I know is wrong, but I don't have the strength to do what is right. Please help me.' That's all I said—tears pouring down my face. I had never felt so weak and helpless—I couldn't find in myself what I needed to do the right thing.

"Helpless"

The day started out bleak and cold.
This was supposed to be a decisive day in my life—a dark day.

I was about to walk into a trap that would haunt me the rest for the rest of my life.
Then I opened my heart and gently pleaded for Your help—
 I was helplessly weak—no strength,
Strength to do the right thing.
As I faced the crowd around me—I knew I didn't belong here.
Then You spoke—a question it was!
You had not left me—You heard my cry for help.
As usual, you came through just when I was at the end of myself—helpless.
You spoke strength into me—
The fact is You have never let me down.
You won't this time—
I don't know what will happen—How the tables will turn.
I know it is a long hard road ahead—Much to contend with.
It's comforting to know You haven't left.

"Grateful Child"

MARCH 17, 2000 (PART 2)

A Defining Moment

As I entered the doctor's office that cold day in March, it was crowded. I was a bit taken aback and felt like I wanted to run. The receptionist behind the desk gave me a clipboard with a form to complete. I sat down and read the first question—How did you hear about us? I immediately heard a clear, distinct voice ask a question:

"Have I ever let you down?" I turned around to see who spoke, but no one was there. Startled, I stood up and gave the receptionist the clipboard with the blank form. I had not written a word. I raced out of the room and down the stairs—I needed air to breathe.

My Father had spoken to me—He had not left me! This was the first time I heard Him in months. I walked out on the streets of Brooklyn overwhelmed with a sense of belonging—I was wanted and loved! He hadn't given up on me! I needed a place to cry, a place where no one would say a word to me. I looked ahead and saw a coffee shop. As I walked up to the door, I looked in—It appeared to be either a Jewish coffee shop or one where they frequented. The customers inside were all religious or orthodox Jewish men dressed in their typical Jewish garbs. I knew they would not say anything to me. This was the place I needed. I ordered a cup of hot chocolate and found a corner, and I cried non-stop. No one even looked at me. This was what I needed—I wouldn't have known what to say to even begin to explain what I was going through. I left the coffee shop when there were no more tears to cry. My Father had intervened and helped me when I had no strength to help myself. What a love! Truly He had never let me down. I knew what He meant—It meant 'child, I got you. I got your back.'

I have pondered this many times and wondered— 'Why me?' I have met different women—single, married, church and unchurched, who had ended their pregnancies and not had that dramatic encounter with the Lord. Why did He intervene to stop me? I don't know if the Lord had spoken to these women. I don't know enough to speak about some of those mysteries in life. All I know is God is sovereign, and He does whatever he chooses to do, whenever He chooses to do it.

Years later, the Lord revealed this truth to me, and I think it has helped bring some measure of clarity to me. When I was a teenager—

just newly in a relationship with Jesus, someone attempted to rape me on my way to a youth meeting at church. Miraculously, the Lord delivered me. Many girls (even in church) have been sexually assaulted. I asked the Lord about it. This is what the Lord revealed to me. He said the things He protected me from are the things I wouldn't have survived—those were the things that would have destroyed me. I wouldn't have survived a sexual assault, and I wouldn't have survived an abortion. Because He made me, I trust that He knows me best. This also means that every difficulty the Lord has allowed in my life has redemptive and refining purposes. These challenges are not meant to destroy me—If He allows it, He has also equipped me with the tools I need to overcome.

> *I can do all things [which He has called me to do] through Him who strengthens and empowers me [to fulfill His purpose—I am self-sufficient in Christ's sufficiency; I am ready for anything and equal to anything through Him who infuses me with inner strength and confident peace.]*
> **Phil 4:13AMP**

REFLECTIONS

3

The Road Ahead

MARCH 18, 2000

Walking into the unknown can be very daunting. I knew the Lord was with me, but that never exempted me from having questions and fears. This was going to be a long, hard road. My personal challenges didn't just disappear when the Lord spoke to me. I was going to have to walk this out in front of my church, my family, and my immediate community of friends and enemies. That was a journey I didn't look forward to.

"Don't Know"

> I still don't know if I can do this—There are moments of deep disappointment.
> How could my life, which was so promising, turn out this way?
> What happened to this dream that every girl has?
> What did I do so horrible that this piece of the puzzle of my life gets worst as the years go by?
> I really do feel a sense of hopelessness—I've disappointed so many,

Including myself, not to mention You—Lord.
I still can't help asking, "Why?"
You knew the disaster that I'd walk right into—the total mess I'd make,
Yet You allowed me to go.
I did not ask to go—You sent me.
I confess I still don't understand.
I'm afraid I can't see past my nose at this point; all I see now is darkness.
I don't know how, when, or why—
I just don't know…
'Questioning Child'

*** There's a part of the story I haven't yet shared. This will probably help to explain the questions I had on this day. You see—I felt led to go to a community for a few months to volunteer my services in another country. This is where I met my son's father. To this day, I still know that the Lord directed me there. Even as I am writing 20 years later—I still don't know why. I still ask why—but from a different place. I also know that I am responsible for the choices I make, and I need to be held accountable. I am not obsessed with getting an answer, as I know I probably never will—and that's okay. I now know some questions may never be answered this side of eternity. When there are no answers, I have learned to trust His hand.

MARCH 21, 2000

Our finite minds tend to grapple with things we don't understand, sometimes to the point of weariness. This was not a good day. I wanted clarity—I wanted the picture perfectly painted for me. I needed to know how I was going to do this—alone. I was looking for a place to cast blame. I was subtly telling God that He knew this would happen—Why didn't He intervene? In retrospect, I know that line of reasoning makes no sense, but that was how I felt. That's one thing I love about God—He allows me to be human. I have always felt I can tell Him exactly what I am feeling—whether those feelings make sense or not. He is not offended. He invites us to 'come now and let us reason together.' I found Him to be my safe place, a place where I can have conversations that might make others uncomfortable. I discovered a judgment-free zone, and I have never felt more free, free to be my authentic self and change as He molds me accordingly.

"Can't Understand"

One day in my life, I guess I'll understand.
I am afraid I've cast the blame on Your omniscience—Who am I to do this?
I've made my choices, and they have sent me on a roller coaster ride downhill.
Who do I blame? I feel sick in my entire being.
I guess I'm confused or depressed—Who knows?
I only have one wish or prayer.
It may not sound right—But that's my gut desire right now.
I don't know that I can come out of this—I really don't have the strength.
I just can't find what I need to do this
Not one more time—Not the aloneness

Not the fears, questions, and pain
Not the embarrassment, shame, and anger
Not the struggles all alone—again!
'Weak Child'

> **People ruin their lives by their own foolishness**
> **and then are angry at the Lord.**
> **(Prov.19:3 NLT)**

MARCH 28, 2000 (PART A)

Sometimes life can lead you to a place where nothing makes sense. On this day, I came to the end of my thoughts, if that makes sense. Tired of thinking. Weary and drained of emotions—I was just "there." Clueless and numb. This was a period when I had gotten very cold and matter of fact. I didn't care much about other people's thoughts or feelings. Sometimes that meant I ignored phone calls, notes, cards sent to me—ignored people. At times I never answered the door. I couldn't think about other people's feelings. I just needed to survive. Do you get that?

"Time Passes By"

I sit here as time passes by
—too drained to even worry.
Depression is not the description of my dilemma.
Having exhausted all emotions—I don't know where to begin or end.

Not sure what I feel daily—I just allow myself to go. As time passes by
I just resolve to do whatever it takes for me to survive.
As seen time and time again—it's always up to me.
There's never anyone really there.
Despite good intentions, the choice is left up to me as always
I'm not sure what I feel or even if that's important.
This is something that I must go through.
I don't know if I possess the strength to.
However, I don't have much of a choice right now.
Where do I go—As time passes by?
'Wondering Child'

LESSONS LEARNED:

I remember battling with the feeling that I had disappointed the Lord in a really bad way. I told Him that quite a few times. One day I heard Him quietly speaking into my spirit: 'You can't disappoint me. Disappointment belongs to humans. You get disappointed because you didn't know or expected something else. I am the All-Knowing God. I knew about your today.' Nothing about us surprises God—He has already made a way for your come-back. When you get to the end of your wondering or wandering, look to Him. You'll find He has been lovingly waiting for you.

MARCH 28, 2000 (PART B)

The noise in your head can become so loud at times that you can't hear the Father's tender whisper. Your heart can be so shut up that you won't even allow Him to love you in His way. Then there are the days when for a moment, you sense the warmth of His love thawing out those cold, embattled places—those places you have closed off. This was one of those moments; for a fluttering minute, I was reminded that as long as my Father is with me and I could start all over again. The ashes and embers of burnt-out dreams can be re-lit. There's life after the fall. For a brief moment, I remembered His ability to redeem and restore.

"Where?"

Where do I go when all else fails?
When the walls come tumbling down
Where do I get the wind for my sails, as my ship rocks in life's storms?
To where do I run when all my run is gone, when I've reached the end of me?
I guess I begin with—YOU.
I feel the jaws of gloom trying to swallow me.
There's little light on all sides.
How I long to feel set free—delivered, I suppose, from life itself.
Where do I begin to get answers?
I guess I begin with all I know—YOU.
I hear there's grace enough ready to pull you through it all.
You know, this one is really tough.
Where do I begin to find the strength to even think or see clearly?
I don't know anything else than to begin with—YOU.
You are all I know when sin overwhelms

You are all I know when nothing makes sense
You are all I know in times of confusion
Where do I begin? I begin with YOU.
'Searching Child'

MARCH 30, 2000

There are days you feel like you are becoming undone. The edges of your mind and emotions are becoming frayed. That which should hold you together continues to elude you. This was one of those days…

"Falling Apart"

I feel like I'm in hell right now!
I don't know what I'll do the next moment.
I have no feeling but one of hopelessness—feeling blank.
I don't know where to begin or even what to do.
I know I'm handling everything inappropriately but
I just don't know where to begin.

LESSONS LEARNED:

Sometimes when it feels like your life is imploding— 'things fall apart; the center cannot hold,' it may just be that God is putting things in place. The shifting and instability we experience at that time can be overwhelmingly uncomfortable and, at times, painful. This is when you feel like you are free-falling and you have no idea whether to come or go.

I found out that the best thing to do in those times is to just rest. Sometimes when you don't know what to do—do nothing but trust. Even when that sense of trust evades you—know that the God with everlastingly strong arms will carry you.

> *When my heart is overwhelmed; Lead me to the rock that is higher than I.*
> *(Psalm 61:2 NKJV)*

MARCH 31, 2000

All of us have a built-in desire to survive. When those desires are driven by misled emotions, we often make poor choices. On this day, I wanted to get away from the familiar—maybe from the very things or people who reminded me of my failure, my imperfections. If I moved to a different place where no one knew me, that might be an easier road to walk down. It's funny how we think that escaping is the answer when God calls us to go through the process. I didn't want to walk this out in front of those who were familiar with my 'better days.' I distinctly remember how I had to take a deep breath as I came close to the doors of my church. Yes, I went to church every week. When it became too much, I considered moving away.

"Weary Soul"

Lord, I'm making this move as long as the door opens. I find it difficult to 'live' right here.
I feel closed in by four walls, almost suffocating.

I need to break loose and start all over. I've not seen so much darkness around me in a long time.

Isn't it funny how we can get to the point where we understand how people can remain in literal 'hell' for years? I guess now I understand the 'lost' and their dilemma much more.

We can always prance around in our 'righteousness,' almost flaunting it in their faces. We can never truly touch them until we 'feel' their bondage.

(Who shall deliver me from this body of death?)

I still know that you love me. I also know it's Your way or not at all. It doesn't matter how much I run or hide—It's only in that secret place that I'll find rest and peace for my soul.

'Needing Rest'

> ***You can make many plans, but the Lord's purpose will prevail.***
> **(Prov. 19:21NLT)**

LESSONS LEARNED:

One thing I struggled with was the chatter around me, real or perceived. This was one of the reasons I had wanted to get away. The truth was, there were more people 'for me than against me.' When you are in a place of pain, your perception can easily get distorted. Guard against the lies of the enemy and your own blurred vision.

One day, I made a comment to Lord after hearing some chatter. The Lord very firmly told me that if I didn't give them 'something to talk about,' they wouldn't be talking. I heard a very firm- 'Grow up!' I never went back to that place. He never protected me from all the chatter either. I needed to develop mental and emotional mettle. This life is not for the 'faint of heart.' He will not always protect us from the uncomfortable. I have come to discover that God is more interested in my character than my comfort. There is such a thing as the 'refiner's fire.

MARCH 31, 2000

I have learned not to make decisions from a place of fear, chaos, or any other unhealthy emotion. What I thought I needed was not what was best for me. Though I felt driven by an intense desire to survive (so I thought), the truth is I had a difficult time walking through the shame and pain. Somehow, I felt if I went to a new place, I could breathe again. The reality is God wanted me to breathe through the pain and sorrow exactly where He planted me. I didn't want to…I didn't think I could.

"Decisions"

> *They (decisions) can be so major at times—life-changing for most. Sometimes the steps needed are drastic, almost revolutionary, even senseless at times.*
> *The need to survive is a very powerful one; it drives you to the point of action*
> *Even in moments when life seems to get stagnant.*
> *Right now, I NEED to survive—mentally, spiritually, and emotionally.*
> *My choices may not be rational or even thoughtful.*
> *I know that God is sovereign—He can change whatever He pleases.*

In my choices, I know it's hard to kick against the prick.
It's either God's way or disaster.
I leave my ways open to Him.
In the meantime, I move as I'm propelled—
Propelled by a need to survive without losing my mind.
'Desperate Child'

LESSONS LEARNED:

As I struggled with wanting to move away, I thought this is the only way I could survive this journey in a mentally healthy way. For some reason, part of me knew that 'God's way is perfect,' and I gave Him the latitude to upend my plans as He saw fit. It's interesting how in your darkest moment, the Christ in you still fights for you—if you give Him space.

One day, my pastor called me into his office and said to me, "Don't run away. If you leave, you will never become who God intended you to be. If you are willing to fight, I will fight with you."

No one in my immediate circle knew my thoughts or plans to move. I never shared this with anyone. I was so taken aback that day—I knew the Spirit of God was intervening to prevent me from making a poor choice. I listened and stayed. I am so glad I did.

You see, I had made a commitment to my Father at the beginning of this journey. I knew it would be a difficult one, and I knew I would not always think or act right. I told Him that He could do whatever He wanted with me as long as He didn't leave me alone. I made up my mind to follow His leading always, as long as I knew it was Him. He will never stop fighting for you, if you let Him.

> *We can make our plans, but the Lord determines our steps.*
> *(Prov. 16:9 NLT)*

JUNE 28, 2000

I have come to learn that I can ask God a question without 'questioning' Him. He is not offended. This path that I traveled was made a little easier because I felt the freedom to talk to God from a raw, vulnerable place. In retrospect, some of these things I wrote were probably laughable or offensive to the ears of everyone one else—except my Father. These seasons allow for true intimacy to be developed between me and the Creator, whose love is limitless. I didn't have to make sense or say the right thing. I only needed to keep the conversation going. That's what we call prayer or spending time with God. I found out that He's not so much looking for me to have on the right clothing, say the right words or have the correct physical posture—he just wants me to talk to Him. Everything else eventually does fall into place. He really just wants 'me'—my heart. So I asked questions…

"I know…"

> *I know my questions may seem out of place.*
> *You'll probably never respond to some of them.*
> *I can't seem to help asking why.*
> *I know I am ultimately responsible for the choices I make.*
> *I know you have taught me well.*
> *I know the power to live or die lies in my decisions.*
> *I know I may not get anywhere asking these 'whys.'*

*I can't seem to help the pain that seers through me at times
So I end up asking why.
Don't hold these seemingly ridiculous cycles of questions against me.
I know you know my heart and only you can search me.
I know you'll ease the pain, even if I never know 'why.'
'Questioning Child'*

LESSONS LEARNED:

Some years ago, I connected with a high school friend. As we did some catching up, he shared a painful piece of his story. As a freshman, his college girlfriend had gotten pregnant. Faced with pressure from her family, she terminated the pregnancy. He had opposed that option but could do nothing about it. When I saw him years later, he had gotten married and had other children. He confessed to me that he never got over it. It took him years to stop mourning over what would have been the child's birth month.

Questions are a part of life—things happen and the whys are real. Sometimes pains are self-inflicted; at times, we suffer because of the choices of others. Either way, the struggle is real and the questions haunt us in deep places. I reflect on Job; I have always been fascinated with the fact that God never explained to Job why he went through his trials. There was a purpose unknown to the natural man. Job had a plethora of questions, but through his emotional ups and downs, he never lost faith in God.

I have learned that being obsessed with the answers to 'why' can be crippling. The song **'Remind Me You're Here'** has become part of my anthem collection. 'The writer penned these words, "I won't ask you for reasons - 'Cause a reason can't wipe away tears." When we don't get the answers, we can trust His hand, His heart, and His purpose. Sometimes the answers will unfold as we give Him the pain that comes with the 'whys.'

AUGUST 1, 2000

Sometimes when you view life through your limited lens, it can look dismal and hopeless. There's the tendency to forget that you are not the sum of your mistakes. You are so much more than what you do or don't do. You can't fall so far that the grace of God can't reach you. This was one of those days when I looked at the ashes around me and lost sight of who God was…

"Déjà Vu"

I look back over my life, and it seems like I've been here before—
The aloneness, the struggle with choices, the fears, and the tears.
I did walk this road of tumult before—a rocky one it was.
My life seems so filled with scars of some sort or another—
Scars from the many bumps and potholes on the road of life.
I really have nothing to be proud of—nothing to boast in
Life seemingly filled with bad choices and horrific consequences
I have much to be ashamed of; seems like I have been here before.
I am really nothing without God's grace—
Seems like I've heard that before too.
Will I get out of this vicious cycle?
This time around, it's hard to get up in the true sense of the word.
Is it going to take years again as it did before?
Is this déjà vu?

LESSONS LEARNED:

When I was in college, I met a very sweet young lady in our Christian fellowship group. Her testimony always touched my heart. She shared that her mother was sexually assaulted and had gotten pregnant. While she was pregnant, she met a man who fell in love with her and they got married. Her mother chose to have the baby. This young lady was that baby. She often shared about the love that her "father" has for her and her him. Through the eyes of this amazing man, she saw the love of her Heavenly Father.

We don't always see how things are going to work out. That is part of what we call the walk of faith. You believe before you see; you trust when you cannot see. It is true that we cannot always 'see, hear, or fathom' the things that God has in store for those who dare to trust Him.

REFLECTIONS

4

Putting the Pieces Back Together

FEBRUARY 18, 2003

This is a few years later. My son was now about twenty-seven months old, a beautiful child. His father had passed away tragically when he was just about five weeks old—they never met. One reason I had contemplated ending the pregnancy was simply because I wanted to get away from his father. Quite selfish in retrospect. He was not a bad person but was very caring and committed to being a father. I just knew this was not God's will for me, nor was it my desire to be part of his life. I felt if we shared a child together, I could not get rid of him. I did not know what God knew. God knew the number of his days—I didn't. His death really took me for a spin—that was another road I had to travel. Now I truly was going to do this alone—or so I felt.

At this point, I had experienced the goodness of God in remarkable ways. He placed people in my life (some were already there) who made this journey so much more manageable. Though my scars were being healed, it continued to be a journey of trust and self-examination. One thing that continued to ring true for me was God's faithfulness and commitment to the process. He truly 'completes the good work' He starts in us (Phil. 1:6). On this day, I reflected on His faithfulness…

"Always"

You always answer my prayers—
It's just at times, I'm not listening.
Too busy maybe, too noisy
To quiet my heart to hear from You—
That above the roars and the crashing of the waves—
I'll know You're always there
Always listening, always answering
You are always waiting to hear my voice.
My heart, my soul, thirsting for You
Always longing for me to draw closer to You
To be one with You.
'Yours Always'

LESSON LEARNED:

I remember as I fought through that very challenging season; many days, I know I was carried. I often looked ahead, trying to get a glimpse of the end. I had many conversations with my Father. It was not uncommon for people to end up bitter, resentful, and cynical after walking through a season like mine. I clearly remembered my prayer:

"Father, I know I will rise from the ashes—I will come out this. When I come out on the other side, I want to have a pure heart. I want to be free from animosity or resentment."

The Lord has been faithful—I came out with a pure heart. I walked through the character-refining moments with grace. I remember the times I was not invited to weddings or baby or bridal showers, birthday parties, etc. On one occasion, in a women's meeting in church, there was a circle prayer with each person praying a short prayer. The sister on my left prayed, then it was my time; the sister on my right started praying before I opened my mouth. I interpreted that to mean that I wasn't supposed to pray. This was just one of the times I had to resist the 'spirit of offense.' I mentioned these things not to cast any negative images on my sisters or brothers but to bring to light the processing that comes with the journey. I don't necessarily think that people were always intentionally trying to pass me over or whatever. Many of us find it very difficult or uncomfortable to deal with people when they 'fall from grace' or going through something traumatic. We don't always know what to say or do. Sometimes it's easier to say nothing for fear we say or do the wrong thing.

I am convinced that God allowed me to walk through all of that so I could see what was in my heart. I had asked for a pure heart; I would be challenged to rise to the occasion when faced with these tests. Of course, I haven't forgotten everything said or done by flawed humans (like myself). However, I remember them with a smile—I truly can laugh at myself. I use them as teaching moments for myself, and I try today to extend as much grace to others as I possibly can—especially to those who are 'going through.'

Trusted with the Process

One Sunday morning in January of 2021, the Lord spoke very quietly to my heart. This was not the first time He had spoken some measure of this truth to me. He said:

As you are getting ready to go to church this morning—there's a young girl going through exactly what you went through 20 years ago. What if I trusted you with the process—for her and the countless others who feel that this is the end? They feel there's no way out of their current situation. This journey was not meant to destroy you—I trusted you with the process.

It's not always about us; this journey is way bigger than our limited scope of thinking. I remember my pastor saying to me, "Don't let this experience go to waste." I don't claim to always understand everything that God chooses to use or even what He allows. For sure, He never leads us into sin; that is not His nature. However, our faithful Father knows how to turn our messes into messages to reach hearts that need it. How and when He does this depends largely on the state of our heart and our response to His corrections. Taking responsibility for our missteps is the beginning. A 'broken and contrite spirit,' He will never abandon or reject *(Psalm 51: 17)*. Consider it an honor to have God trust you not to jump out of the fire but to stay faithful in the flames. Someone is waiting to hear how you did it.

In the crucible of affliction, the flawed me began to be refined to look more like the One who loved me enough to not let me go. The One who trusted me enough to lead me through. He knew I would stay committed to the process.

5

Lessons from My Father

GOING BACK

I have learned that prayer is never a substitute for repentance. Sometimes our sins are very obvious to the eyes, and sometimes they are not. I had confessed my sins and turned away, or so I thought. Somewhere in the midst of the 2020 pandemic, like many others, I paused to do a lot of soul searching. One day I was praying for my son – "storming the gates of hell or heaven," not sure which one. For some reason, mothers take on a warrior stance when our children appear to be out of sync with what we perceive their purpose to be. This was one of those days. As I started to speak life over my son's destiny, I heard a calm voice: "Did you forget that you were the first one who wanted to kill him? Not the enemy."

I was stunned. I thought to myself, *But I didn't have the abortion. What sin did I commit?* The Lord quietly corrected me, like a loving father. Even though I did not have the abortion, I needed to renounce my act of entertaining the thought to kill my son. That day, twenty years later, I had to go back in the realms of the spirit to correct a wrong I had agreed with and taken steps to carry out. I am not saying we need to go into panic mode trying to remember every wrong thought we entertained. If you are like me, there have been many sins—too many to remember. I am saying that when we give God our hearts, He will by His Spirit bring to light those that we need to renounce individually. There is such a thing as closing doors that would otherwise give access to the enemy. We would be surprised by the doors we unknowingly open at times by our actions and thoughts. Thankfully, we have a loving Father who helps us to navigate this life in the spirit realm.

I encourage us to pay attention to those subtle nudges and whispers of the Spirit. We don't always understand the ways of God, nor do we always understand how things work in the spirit (***Isaiah 55: 8-9***). I have learned that this walk as a child of God is far more spiritual than it is physical. I don't understand it all, and I don't have to understand it all. I find that if I trust my Father's hand and voice, He will never lead me wrong.

Part of my healing and recovery involved apologizing to those I hurt in the process. God has a way of always taking us back to first things first. He loves us too much to allow us to get by without correcting us. I remember a sister sharing her story with me many years ago. She was married and not happy with the way things were in her marriage. She had gotten pregnant at some point during those difficult days. She ended the pregnancy without her husband's knowledge. My "sister" felt she could not carry a child into that situation at the time. I remembered part of the conversation that ensued. Certainly, I was in no position to condemn her. I did understand because I was just there a few weeks before. There I go but for the grace of God. I also knew God did not endorse that act and that she couldn't have been in the best place in her walk with Christ. I told her that God might one day require her to go back and confess that to her husband. I don't know if she ever did. As a cautionary note, I am not advocating that we need to confess everything to everyone. Use the wisdom of God and let Him guide you with the what, who, when, and how. The Father I know loves us too much to leave us undone. Like surgery, going back to renounce, denounce, confess, and ask for forgiveness can be painful but necessary for our health as a whole person.

Extra Grace Required

When we fall from grace, others are affected in the process—people who look up to us, our family, our church, and our friends. Their response to our failures can range from undying support, to confusion, to disappointment, to withdrawal. People are people—flawed and complicated. Like us, they will talk and won't always act right! It is in our nature to get defensive, resentful, and at times even combative. Remember, we did the sinning. Although no one is perfect, right now, we are in the wrong. It's good to take a posture of humility as we journey through the healing process. Submitting to the Potter's hand allows the refining process to take place with less pain.

A few weeks after it was publicly known that I was pregnant, a young lady stopped by to see me. She had recently started her walk with Christ and would often share with me. She looked up to me. I had disappointed her, and she was a bit confused. I don't quite recall every detail of the conversation, but I remember her sharing how she felt. I listened and reassured her that though I had failed, I had not walked away from Christ. I admitted my wrongdoing and asked forgiveness for not being a better example to her. I then reminded her that she could not use my failure as an excuse when she stands before Christ. She was responsible for her own walk with Christ. It doesn't matter who falls away—Christ died for her and made provisions for her to "stand, and having done all things to remain standing." I shared this not to debate whether she was wrong or right to come to me. Either way, it doesn't matter—I have found that I shouldn't judge people's reactions in these situations. Only God truly knows the intent of people's hearts. Many times, God allows these encounters so we can see the state of our own hearts. Can we respond with grace rather than arguing about whether someone's action is right or wrong?

I have taken to heart one piece of advice over the years—look for the best and expect the worst. This has saved me from a lot of disappointment. I have come to realize that the only response I can control is my own. People will surprise you in many ways. This is the time to give extra grace to yourself and others.

Letting God Love You

The state of our heart is important in the sight of God. Even though I was going to church through all of this, my heart was very guarded. I tried to protect myself from the chatter, real or imagined. Always remember the enemy of our soul uses divisiveness as one of his tools. His way is to divide, isolate, and conquer. When you are in this state, you tend to believe that everyone is talking about you. Don't buy this lie! That is not always true. Believing this lie can be crippling and a hindrance to your recovery. The Scriptures warn us not to be "ignorant of his devices."

During my darkest moments, sometimes I would visit Brooklyn Tabernacle's Tuesday night prayer meeting. I had attended BT for a season in the 1990s, and this was one of my favorite services there. I would visit when I needed a place where no one looked at me—no one knew me. One night, the leader asked us to turn to the person to our right and pray for that person. A young lady next to me held me and prayed with me. I literally felt God's arm wrapped around me—not asking me for anything, just loving me. I never saw that young lady again, but God used her that night to express His love to me in an amazing way. I'll never forget that experience. God loves us through people, if we allow Him.

As I sat in church one day with a group of women, my heart still guarded, I heard a very quiet whisper: "Why don't you let me love you through them?" This was when my heart started to melt. Of course, the change did not happen all at once; it was a journey of love and trust. I am still in that same church today. This is where I serve in leadership. They watched my fall and my rise from the ashes. The road has been quite eventful but filled with many beautiful moments.

One of my college girlfriends was sexually assaulted, had gotten pregnant, and carried the baby. She literally went to hell and back. When we reflected on our journey, she shared about the dark place that she found herself during that season. She would tell you that no one but Jesus carried her through. She also shared how God later blessed her with a great husband who helped restore the broken places in her life—a man who loved her gently and hard. The love of God is a healing balm for the wounds and scars life brings. This love flows through His people. God still uses people to help love us back to wholeness.

The Unfathomable Love of God

The love of God gives 100%. He loves—risking rejection. We ignore Him for years and still, His love remains stubborn. We put Him last on our list of priorities so often, but when we sincerely call out to Him, he shows up. He does not throw our past failures and mistakes in our faces. He doesn't constantly remind us of the foolish choices we've made.

Every day with Him is a new chance to start over. He is not afraid to give me another chance even after I've messed up the one hundredth time. He is not quick to judge me when I don't think or act right. He is more concerned about the condition or motives of my heart. His plans are always redemptive—He never intends to harm. Even when He gets tough with me, His love for me is always so evident. He truly gets me! O to love like He loves!

Never Roll Over

Scripture reminds us to "fight the good fight of faith." Some seasons carry with it unceasing battles. Sometimes when it rains, it pours. To truly walk into your divine destiny, quitting can never be an option. On some days, that's all you might want to do. Be very alert because the enemy will do everything in his power to help you achieve that end. He is good at bombarding us with lies and suggestions. Always remember to filter your thoughts through the Word of God. If God doesn't endorse it in His Word, then we don't want to entertain or dwell on that thought.

On one of my darkest days, I remember walking into my bathroom and looking in the mirror. I looked closely at my eyes and almost did not recognize the person I saw. The sadness I saw was unreal. As I stood there feeling sorry for myself—I heard a very sharp voice almost shouting at me, "Why don't you just roll over and die?" Immediately, the Spirit in me rose up, almost in defiance. I shouted to the mirror, "I shall not die, but live and declare the works of the Lord!"

At that moment, I realized that self-pity gives the enemy room to speak his lies. No one ever says that the road back is an easy one. When God poured His Spirit into us, He gave us divine enablement to do things and deal with situations we could never handle on our own. He is for us, not against us. Fight on—never roll over and die! In our weakest moments, His strength is made perfect.

REFLECTIONS

6

A Work in Progress

THE WORK CONTINUES

As I attempt to give others a glimpse into my journey, I want to point out that although I have come a long way—the work continues. The struggle is real! There is a continuous peeling away of the layers I had consciously or subconsciously used to mask the pain of the human experience. I believe God, in His mercy, does this one layer at a time. I sense that we are not always ready for the stripping away. Some things are buried so deeply, especially those associated with our childhood experiences, only the Holy Spirit can bring true awareness.

Even as I pen these words, I must confess that I still deal with shame and a sense of disappointment at times. I still have to bathe my mind in the truth of God's words to win daily. I wasn't aware that I was battling shame. I had succeeded in masking it with "doing." I pushed myself to go to grad school and position myself to take care of business. I was not looking for anyone to take care of me. I had placed a protective layer over me, unknowingly hiding my shame of being a single mother.

One evening, I sat in church, being a good churchgoer. I heard in my spirit, "Be careful of the reason you want to get married. Are you sure it's not to hide your shame?" Of course, I started reasoning in my head. I didn't think I had a problem with shame. On the outside, I looked confident, self-assured, and poised. That was not my problem. No one knows our inner self like the Lord does. He knows the real me, the real you—not the one we create to face the unforgiving world we live in.

As I continued to wrestle with this new revelation, a scene from my childhood flashed before my eyes. I don't remember how old I was, but my mother was pregnant with one of my siblings. At that time, my mother was living with her current husband, but they were not yet married. Her sister was very bold and spoke her mind willingly. She seemed to have an issue with my mom having "all these children" and not being married. She always made that known when she visited. Knowing what I know now, my mother must have wanted to get married. She acted like it wasn't a big deal. Maybe it wasn't an issue for my stepfather, but I'm sure my mother wanted to get married.

One day, my aunt was visiting. I knew my mom was pregnant again, and for some reason, I was watching to see how my aunt would react. My mom never told her she was pregnant. It appeared to me that my mom was hiding her pregnancy. As a little girl, I watched my mother closely. I could see she was ashamed, and I couldn't quite describe what I felt that day—maybe anger. Who was I angry at? I'm not sure. That is the scene that flashed across my memory that day in church. I don't remember ever dwelling on that event at any point in my life. Why did that image come to my mind at that moment? As I pondered this, the Lord revealed to me that the spirit of shame was transferred to me that day. I had made a decision that I would not be like my mom in that sense. Yet here I was—a single mom!

I have confessed it and so many times felt like I had moved past it, but then it pops up again. I think I still battle with some residue ever so often. I have always worked with educational professionals, most of whom have had their children in wedlock. I find myself still hesitant to reveal that I was never married when my children were born. I tend to keep away from those conversations. I'm still walking through this, and I know the story will continue to unfold. He who "began the good work in me will complete it" **(Phil. 1:6)**. I believe other layers within me need to be peeled away so I can be the best version of the me that God intended.

Secret Shame

I found this note in one of the places where I journaled over the years. I don't remember if I wrote it or copied it from someone or somewhere, but I think it is worth repeating. Based on John 4:

> **The shame that causes you to go to the well at a time when no one else is there. You avoid getting close or vulnerable. You avoid certain conversations or you talk religious. You get religiously defensive. Then you meet someone who sees beyond the facade and actually cares about you and your mess. He forces you to own and confront your failures and shortcomings and then lets you know he loves you just the same. My shame now becomes my story…the platform upon which I stand to proclaim Christ's unconditional love.** *(1/16/2016 at 1:34 am)*

Our failures can be used as tools in God's kingdom. The enemy tries to use them as yokes to keep us in bondage. You are not "less than" because of your failures, nor are you disqualified. The enemy uses this frequent lie as a dart to keep God's children stagnant and crippled. Scripture reminds us that we "overcome by the blood of the Lamb and the word of our testimony."

"Everyone will share the story of Your wonderful goodness; they will sing with joy about your righteousness" (Psalm 145:7 NLT).

Walk Again

One day you might forget the pain of the past. When God blesses you even in the land of your affliction and you rise above the shattered pieces of your dreams, you forget the shame and begin to dream again. The challenge for some who have stood up after a fall is how to walk again. The Lord spoke this to my heart a few years ago, "There are many who have risen up but haven't begun walking." Many sit in church wearing a garb of religiosity. No passion for anything. Sitting with gifts and talents hidden, many because of fear. Some cannot seem to forget the past. It is one thing to mess up before you confess Christ; it is a whole different story to mess up publicly after you have confessed Christ. Unless you have walked that road, you have no idea of the burden that comes with that. Much of the battle is in the mind. There is a reason the Scriptures speak about the renewing of the mind. This is a great battlefield. I have found that bathing your mind in the Word of God is the first step in winning this battle. The truth of God's Word sets you free. What He says about you and who He says you are to Him are truths that keep you anchored when you are assaulted with the enemy's lies. He will tell you (sometimes you will tell yourself) what you cannot do or become. No doubt, you will be reminded of your past; it comes with the territory. We fight back with, "It is written!"

Unless we begin to walk again, our purpose and destiny are left unfulfilled. Lives are left untouched, songs are left unsung, lessons are left untaught, our worship is silenced, our praise is muffled, and our spirits are left crippled. We must walk again for all who will come behind us, waiting to see us rise, cheering us on, holding our hands. Do it boldly or do it afraid—alone or with a crowd. The Almighty God, the Creator of the Universe, is on our side, and He bids us to come and do life with Him—walk with Him.

REFLECTIONS

Special Dedication

(For my sisters near and far—we are not so different. The paths we walk may be different, but the struggles are all real. The same God who loves me loves you.)

One morning, I sat on an NYC subway car for a 40-minute ride to work. A few minutes into the journey, I noticed a young lady sitting across the aisle from me. She appeared to be talking to herself or someone who was not there. She was nicely dressed but appeared to be just on the verge of losing it. On that crowded number 2 train, I thought about what could have gotten her to this point. What were her struggles? Did she know that she had a Father who wanted to do life with her? Did she know her Father desired her to overcome and walk whole? Did she know…? I took out a pen and a piece of paper and wrote as I watched her. Have you ever felt like you were "on the verge…"?

On the Verge

Just another oppressed mind
Yearning to be set free.
She has struggled long and hard
Realizing nothing is a guarantee.
She tried the men, tried the friend
All a big letdown in the end.

Didn't she know the way out?
Did anyone tell her what it's all about?
It's not how many battles you fight
It's learning to stand in His might.
It's not about whether you win or lose
The victory is in allowing Him to choose.

Cast on Him all your cares.
Your greatest enemy is at times your fears.
They take captive your mind
While you search...peace you can't find
Leaving you hopelessly bound
Wondering where can help be found.

Amazingly He was all you need
He loved you enough to preserve your seed.
Today you can run to Him
Even when all hope seems dim.
He'll lead you into the light
Granting you renewed sight.

O that you may truly see
He's the only one who can set you free!

"For that sister on the #2 train this morning" 3/28/03

SPECIAL DEDICATION

In 2003, as I spoke to myself a thousand times, I had to push through the clouds of doubt and fear that hovered over me ever so often. I'd tell myself that I was equipped for the battle—that I could do this. Thoughts of defeat and shame would still plague me—I had to learn how to fight God's way. I couldn't prevent the birds from flying over my head, but I sure could prevent them from making a nest there. This was a frequent saying my bishop would quote. The battle raged in my mind from time to time. I started fighting like a Christian. On one of these days in 2003, I penned these words.

If

If you can stand strong
When all the walls around crumble
If you can still believe
Even when all hope is lost
Then you can…

If you can rise and walk
After falling the millionth time
If you can see things that are not
As though they were
Then you can…

If you can love again
After another love lost
If you dare to walk in the dark
Knowing your Father is with you
Then you can…

If you can trust Him with your bitter experiences
Allowing Him to make your life sweet
If you can let your spirit rule
Despite your overwhelming desires
Then you can …

If you can believe that this is just a test
And the best is yet to come
Then you can…
You can make it through
You can be all God made you to be!

One evening, I came home from work feeling very worn and tired. It might have been a Friday evening—we had a women's meeting. I didn't feel like saying or doing much. I sat in the back of the sanctuary, and for some reason, my eyes started glancing around the room. We knew each other's story, and every sister had one. As I sat there, an overwhelming sense of admiration and gratitude filled my heart. I started to write some of what stirred in my heart at the moment—I finished it a few days later. Even though my sisters were all walking through their unique situation, they showed up. Shouts of praise and laughter filled the room—most of our situations would remain the same when we left the meeting that night. For those few hours, however, we came together—iron sharpening iron. We were 'sister girls,' doing this together. I encourage all my 'sister girls'—You do not have to do this alone!

SPECIAL DEDICATION

Sister Girl

Sister girl, you overcame for every Hannah
Who was told she couldn't birth a prophet and a priest
While being called barren and no good.
You rose up for every fallen princess
Who was told to "stay down"
You'd never amount to anything.

Sister girl, you endured for every wife
Who was told to quit and walk away
After suffering years of abuse and neglect.
You prayed long enough, hard enough
Fought against all odds
To see your God-given covering rise
Rise to take his rightful place in the kingdom of God.

Sister girl, you birth a true man of God on your knees
Refusing to get up from the birthing position
Until you saw the goodness of the Lord
In the land of the living.

You saw your man rise to greatness
You saw your son walk into his God-given purpose
You saw your grandson finally meeting the lover of his soul
You saw your nephew walk out of his bondage
You saw your father renew his youth like the eagles
You saw your uncle shaking off the shackles that crippled him for years
You saw grandpa increasing in strength even as his earthly tabernacle fails.

Sister girl, you walked out of shame, for every "woman at the well"
Who is searching for "that thing that cannot satisfy."
You became a testimony for every woman "caught in the very act."
You threw off the grave clothes of harlotry
Replaced it with His garment of righteousness
And ... Aren't you looking good!

You were brave for every Esther, Rebekah, or Deborah
Who did what they had to do for the sake of the "Call"
The call to guard the righteousness of God
The call to stand and declare, "If I perish...I perish."
And yes, even for the Rahabs who don't know as yet
That God can and wants to use the less than perfect
To cleanse, break, and mold them in His image.

Sister girl, you stood strong for the daughters of the land
The daughters who were watching....
Watching to see if you could rise from the ashes of your failure
Dust off yourself, strengthen your feeble knees, and walk again.
You became the example of caution
Shouting a warning cry, "A detour from the pathway is dangerous!"
Stay on the narrow pathway; wide is the road that leads to destruction!

You gave hope to a frail heart who could not forgive herself
A beautiful flower who still feels so worthless, so defiled
Even after Christ forgave her.
You encouraged the wounded heart who could not receive
Nor respond to the love of her Perfect Father.

SPECIAL DEDICATION

Your restoration gave a ray of hope to her darkened world
Stirring the "fighting spirit" in a soul
That laid dormant for too long.

Sister girl, you did it when they said you couldn't
You did it afraid until you were bold as a lion.
You refused to give in to the "me" in you that opposed the will of God
You 'pulled' the good out of you while fighting your very self and every demon from hell
You beat your body, soul, and spirit into subjection
Yearning to see "Christ fully formed" in you.

You didn't just go through for you alone—
You endured the valley for those
Who will encounter dream killers, bug depositors, and kingdom scatterers.
You showed us how to win, even when victory seemed so uncertain.
You held on, for the fearful, the unbelieving, the weak, the babe
And yes! Even the hopeful carnal
Cause you've been there, done that!

You persevered for all who will come behind you
Those for whom the valley experience is a daunting one.
Those who dread trials and testing, afraid of the fire.
You allowed the refiner's fire to process you
Until you came out "as pure gold."

You climbed out of the valley when the King beckoned you to arise
Like a lady, you walked across the stage of life with your head held high.

Sister girl, this is your moment…your summer…your new thing!
Play the role—walk into purpose, walk into newness, walk into your destiny!
This is your day; you overcame!

(Dedicated to all sisters who have gone through, are still going through, those who will go through, those afraid of going through…I stand with you) *5/24/05 12:50pm.*

Many times, *girls like me* who haven't traveled the road of restoration in a healthy, godly way sometimes leave a trail of hurt and pain behind us. Hurting, scarred people do not always relate to others in the best way. We tend to carry baggage that we can unload on those who are the closest and dearest to us. This was the story of a friend of mine—He inspired this prayer.

In 2005-2006, my friend 'Mike' found himself in a dark and dismal place, disappointed with some women in his life, including his mother. We chatted for hours. His emotions were so intense I felt like the situation was beyond me. I felt like my words to him were merely like strips of bandages covering up a nasty wound. One issue he was dealing with was his mother not telling him who his father was. He was in his forties and didn't know who his father was.

There was a woman *(a girl like me)* who could not tell her son the truth. I often reflect on her 'why.' Why could she not tell her son the truth? What shame, pain, disappointment, or even anger had she buried deep in the inner recesses of her being? The reality is, she may never tell him the truth. I understand where she is. That could have been me. Girls like me have those places barricaded off—few, if anyone, may enter. These are the places that Jesus desires to visit, those hidden places. He alone can bring the wholeness that girls like me hunger for.

I felt "Mike's" pain—I felt helpless. I connected him with my pastor, who was better equipped to minister to him in places I couldn't. Then I went to my Father with this prayer:

Man After Your Own Heart

Make his soul a well-watered garden
Cause the barren places within him to flourish
Shore up the fault lines, called weaknesses, in his structure
Transform his thought process to be like Yours
Re-define who he is
Make him a man after Your own heart.

Channel his energy into those things that have an eternal value
Lead him to streams in the desert
Purify his being of that which taints and perverts
Grant him a God-given perspective of his manhood
Create within him a wellspring of praise
Make him a man after Your own heart.

Cause him to triumph over present adversities
Declare him a victor over his past failures
Like an eagle, may he soar above the trifling distractions of this life
Keep him unpolluted from that which comes to corrupt
Birth new visions within his spirit constantly
Make him a man after Your own heart.
Set him apart for Your own doings

Position him in his place of authority
Deliver him from a stagnant and unfruitful life
Plant his feet in your perfectly designed plan
Make him a man after Your own heart.

May Your perfect love replace the fears in him
Grant that what he yearns for will be aligned to Your desires
Sustain him when he feels parched within
Carry him when he is weighed down in his soul
Renew his youth when added strength is needed
Make him a man after Your own heart.

Awake the warrior within him
Teach him how to wield his sword
Guard his body, soul, and spirit from frequent wanderings
Surround him with those who will speak life into his situations
Let him be a channel of blessing to the lives he will touch
May your Word be the tool that defines who he is
Make him a man after Your own heart.

> "This prayer is for all the men and boys who have been hurt and scarred by girls like me."
>
> Marcia A. Yetman

SPECIAL DEDICATION

Recently, I was reminded to celebrate my wins more often. I join with my sisters (and brothers) who have made strides on the road to recovery. You have seen the goodness of God in the land of the living. Your todays are much better than your yesterdays. There is hope for tomorrow as you walk hand in hand with your Father. This is for you:

For You

The days were not always what you wanted them to be
Sometimes you found yourself in dry and barren places
The temptation to complain sometimes confronted you
Like a warrior, you sometimes fought to preserve your sense of self
But.... you made it!

You faced challenges of varying sorts
Family tragedies and triumphs
Personal failures and successes
Like a fearful child, you may have faced some dark places
But.... you made it!

Some questions were left unanswered
Broken relationships....no closure as yet
Many nights silence was your companion
Chapters in the pages of your life still not completed
But.... you made it!

Life taught you many unwelcome lessons
Things you had not bargained for
The tapestry of your life woven with many uncertainties

At times you walked away misunderstood and under-appreciated
But.... you made it!

You are still learning to embrace the wonderful mix called life
It's still hard to take the lower ground at times
To give up your rights for the sake of the greater good
Still learning the beauty there can be in silence
But.... you made it!

A wise king once penned, "There is a time for everything under the sun."
I pray this will be the season you will be strengthened by your trials
Blessed to walk on through the times of doubt and fears
This will be your season to step into that prepared place
With confidence, you will speak into your soul...I will make it!

12/20/07 2:40pm

REFLECTIONS

www.ingramcontent.com/pod-product-compliance
Lightning Source LLC
Chambersburg PA
CBHW030351100526
44592CB00010B/921